GREAT INSPIRATIONS

by a Few Great Kids

TRINA DAWKINS PATTERSON

with contributions from a few great kids

Illustrated and designed by Christal Liberatore

Great Inspirations by a Few Great Kids
Copyright © 2013 Trina Dawkins Patterson

Illustrated and designed by Christal Liberatore.
www.christaldesigns.com

Printed in the United States of America.

ISBN-13:978-0615841083
ISBN-10:0615841082

Published by:
TCM
P.O. Box 28051
St. Paul, MN 55128

THE
COOKIE
MOVEMENT
ENRICHING THE LIVES OF WOMEN AND YOUTH

To order, contact The Cookie Movement, LLC.
www.thecookiemovement.com
Books can also be purchased through Amazon.com.

It is easier to build strong children than to repair broken men.

— Frederick Douglass

You are braver than you believe, stronger than you seem, and smarter than you think.

— Christopher Robin from Winnie the Pooh

To all the young writers who graciously and enthusiastically contributed to this book, thank you for lending your voices, your creative thoughts and ideas, and your calls to action. Thank you for being brave enough to share your fears, challenges, and disappointments all in the name of inspiration. Thank you for your messages that will teach, inspire, and encourage young people and the young at heart all over the world.

A special thank you to the parents and guardians of these insightful, kind, and humorous children. Your hard work shines brightly through the pages of this book and is a reflection of the values you have instilled in your children. It is evident that you have planted and watered seeds of faith, hope, and compassion in the hearts of these youngsters. This beautiful project would not have been possible without all of you.

From my heart to yours, thank you.

The Few Great Kids...

Name   Page

You can never go wrong when you are kind, and respect is never out of place.

Kindness...Friendship...Good Character...Being Brave....

Friends are like frosting on a
cake, and I LOVE frosting!

— Summer S., Age 11

I always ask people how they are doing. If they are having a bad day, I try to make their day just a little better with a good conversation.

— Donnell R., Age 16

You're not supposed to do the right thing just for a treat or to get into heaven; you do the right thing because it's the right thing to do.
— Trenton P., Age 12

My Wiggly Tooth

One day I had a wiggly tooth. I could not wait for it to come out. I wiggled it and wiggled it but it would not come out. I was sad, frustrated, and annoyed.

Finally, my dad pulled it out. I showed it to my mom, and she got scared. I felt awesome because at first it hurt when my dad pulled it out but I was brave. The best part was that I got money from the tooth fairy!

— Mia B., Age 7

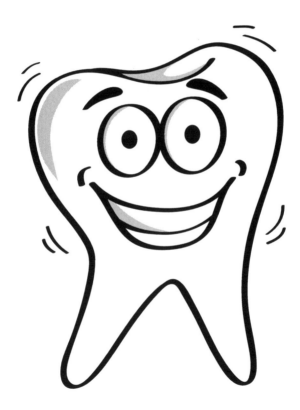

Mom and Dad always say - Birds of a feather flock together, so pick your friends wisely.

— Jordan D., Age 10

Give everyone a chance... especially the lonely kids.

— Noah S., Age 13

If I could go back in time, I would tell myself "change is for the best". In 6th grade, I found out my best friend since kindergarten would be on a different team. I thought it was the worse day of my life. By the second week of school, I found another best friend, and that turned out to be one of the best weeks of my life!

— Jasmine W., Age 11

We're best friends...yeah, baby!
— Clara F., Age 8

Be the best friend you can be and never leave anyone out. How would you feel if you were left out?

— Tacherra E., Age 11

I believe everyone should be treated equally. There should be no saying "you can't play with me" or "you can't sit with me", just because someone may look different, talk different, dress different—it doesn't matter. Be kind to one another and have fun.

—Shayla S., Age 11

I like to help people, a lot!

— Samone Marie C., Age 7

My Brother the Soldier

My brother just returned home from Africa after a one-year tour of duty. I am really looking forward to seeing him because I missed him so much. He is a brave soldier, and he serves our country. I love my brother.

— Keairra P., Age 13

If someone is lonely, I would ask them if they wanted to play with me. Nobody wants to be lonely.

— Sydney S., Age 9

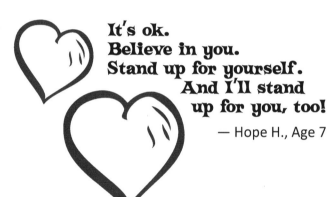

It's ok.
Believe in you.
Stand up for yourself.
And I'll stand
up for you, too!

— Hope H., Age 7

A kind word on a bad day is like
a mother's kiss on a skinned knee.

It makes you feel so much better.

Don't worry...I can help you.
— Imani C., Age 6

I really like the way heaven made you.
—Clara F., Age 8

Adrian's Summer Camp Fun!

I was a good boy at camp today.
I played basketball.
I did a rap song.
I ate an orange at camp today.
I had fun—hip-hip-hooray!

— Adrian J., Age 6

I like playing baseball and being part of a team because my teammates cheer me on and help me when I'm stuck.

— Gabe L., Age 9

If you see somebody being bullied, get involved by standing up and helping out. Tell a parent, guardian, or a teacher. They will fix it. I once was bullied and it was hard, but if you stand up to the bully and tell a teacher, you can make a difference. CHANGE BULLYING! BULLYING IS WRONG! HELP MAKE IT STOP!

It takes a brave person to help stop bullying.

— Antaycia R., Age 10

OBSTACLES ARE OPPORTUNITIES TO SHOW YOUR TRUE CHARACTER

If the fruit is too sour, make it sweet. There will be a time in school when someone may not like you or you may have a problem with someone, and the situation is sour. Always show love, and it will sweeten the situation.

— Marisa G., Age 9

If you had a best friend and she moved away, I would be extra nice to you because I know you would be very sad.

— Sydney S., Age 9

I will play with you.

— Imani C., Age 6

When people are sad, I cheer them up.

— Samone Marie C., Age 7

Talk to somebody new every day.
— Noah S., Age 13

What I love about meeting new people is that they don't know where you came from, and I don't know where they came from. When you meet, it's just a culmination of your life and theirs coming together. They can't judge you on your past because they don't know it—they only see the person life has made you.

— Donovan P., Age 16

I Am...

I am from a home full of love.
    A place where respect is important.
    A town with tight-knit families.
I am from the idea that all things are possible.
    A belief in salvation and redemption.
    The value that compassion is necessary.
I am from a family of creative people.
    Strong friendships.
    Stronger people.
I am from the belief in hope.
    In justice.
    In peace.
I am smart.
    Brave.
    Curious.
I believe I can achieve.

                — George H., Age 15

There is no elevator to success;
you have to take the stairs.

Success…Perseverance…Following Your Dreams….

Carry yourself like royalty.
Royalty is being like a king or queen.
When you are royalty, you can be amused by the court jester.
But you can't be led by him.

— Donovan P., Age 16

WHEN YOU HAVE DONE YOUR BEST, YOU HAVE NOT FAILED — NO MATTER THE OUTCOME

Mom and Dad always say - Do what you have to do now, so that you can do what you want to do later.

— Jordan D., Age 10

Start creating little habits at a young age to prepare for the future.

— Mark B, Jr., Age 16

I am fearfully and wonderfully made.
Psalm 139:14

If you feel like the hill is too hard to climb, look within yourself and know that there will be many hills, but God created you for greatness, so just take one step at a time.

— Makayla G., Age 12

I **CAN** run with my wheelchair;
I just push my wheels extra fast!

— Manny H., Age 3 (Spina Bifida)

THE BEST THING YOU CAN GIVE IS YOUR BEST

Don't let the day make you—
make the day.
— Torri W., Age 13

No matter what obstacles
come your way, the best
way to overcome them is
to pray, smile, reflect on
the situation and push on.
— Zarea F., Age 16

As a student, you have the power to decide your fate. Take charge of it and grasp it while it's still in your reach.

— Morgan T., Age 15

Chase your dreams and never let them go. If you see the direction you want to go and believe in yourself, you can achieve.

— Guyon S., Age 17

You can't say the sky is the limit if
there are footprints on the moon!
— Paul Brandt, Musician

REACH HIGHER

Walk around the world like you own it!

— Tatum M., Age 12

All our **dreams** can come true if we have the **courage** to pursue them.

— Walt Disney

Don't follow the crowd…
— Austin J., Age 11

Keep your head up, always!
— Danielle L., Age 17

EVEN when things get HARD, NEVER QUIT!

My papa always tells me that a winner never quits and a quitter never wins.

— Lewis Adolphus R., Age 12

Don't ever let someone else tell you what you are capable of doing or what you can achieve. If you really want to achieve something, the only person who can stop you from reaching your goal is you.

— Donnell R., Age 16

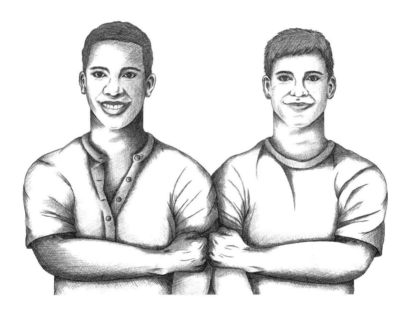

For me, being successful in high school means staying focused.

— Tre' A., Age 15

Why can a little ant carry something that weighs more than 50 times its body weight?

Because he *believes* he can—believe in yourself. You can do great things.

*Be patient and wait—don't just wait
for the ebb, look for the flow.*

Don't sit around expecting hard times, anticipate the carefree times and enjoy them when they come!
— Gunner H., Age 14

You are a flower planted on the earth
ready to bloom with greatness.

Keep your eyes on the future; don't focus on things in the past that may have knocked you down.

— Markita D., Age 14

Life is like a roller coaster: it goes up and down and has loops and turns. Sometimes you want to scream and get off, but when it's all said and done you just want to keep riding.

— Nena A., Age 13

Never give up; there's always a way out.

— Devyn W., Age 16

Just One Life

You have but one time to be young, one time to be old, and one time to die. There are no second chances, no redoes, and no extra lives— you only get one. But there is a secret to getting extra life, and I'm willing to share it with you. All you have to do is make your mark in the world. Work hard to do something amazing, life changing, or a game changer. It might impact one person or a billion people, but no matter what, they will remember you, and you will live forever.

— Guyon S., Age 17

Better to do **something** imperfectly
than to do *nothing* perfectly.

— Robert H. Schuller

To be yourself in a world that is constantly trying to make you something else is the greatest accomplishment.

— Ralph Waldo Emerson

Faith......Self-Discovery......Being Yourself

Make time for the quiet moments because God whispers when the world is loud.

The day I lost my shyness is the same day I found the real me. In middle school, I learned not to be afraid to speak to new people. The more I did it, the easier it became, and the more friends I made. Those friendships helped me discover myself.

— Jabari W., Age 16

You should always be the best **YOU** that you can be, because nobody can tell you that you are doing it wrong.

— Tacherra E., Age 11

By THE WAY...

YOU are pretty AWESOME!

****

I think God made me in the middle of my two brothers so that I can help them.

— Lainey H., Age 6 (sister to two brothers with special needs)

In a message to students and athletes:

Even when it seems bad, it is not **that** bad. Just do your best to make it better.

- Jacqie Carpenter
  CIAA Commissioner

I was always taught you can't go to
an orange grove looking for apples.
— Carrietta D., Age 15

Nobody can make you feel inferior without your permission.

— Zarea F., Age 16

When you don't know what to do, PRAY, and do your best.

— Alaina E., Age 8

Lord, please keep my family safe, day and night.
Amen.

— Xavier S., Age 5

I feel my guardian angels all around me; they keep me safe and warm.

— Jordan W., Age 8

Be the person you would want your kids to be.

— Tatum M., Age 12

Be...
    Brave enough to be yourself.
    Bold enough to love who you are.
    Big enough to not sweat the small stuff.

People see you for who you are, so be yourself.
— Mikayla W., Age 11

The one thing I love about God is EVERYTHING!
— Donovan P., Age 16

*You were designed with a plan
and created for a purpose.*

Extra Special...Extra Special...Extra Special...Extra Special

Watch out world, here I come!
— Emma B., Age 8 (Autism)

Some people call me "different", and some people call me "strange"; some people have even called me "weird". But I don't care because I call myself "**unique**" and that makes me "*special*"...and I like me that way.

— Sunny M., Age 17 (Attention Deficit Disorder and Obsessive-Compulsive Disorder)

I KNOW I can, even though you don't THINK I can.

— Shawnie D., Age 11 (Down Syndrome)

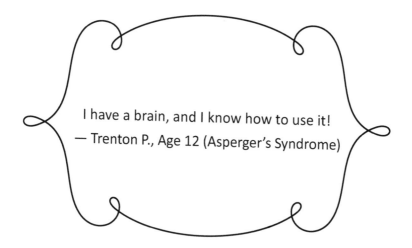

I have a brain, and I know how to use it!
— Trenton P., Age 12 (Asperger's Syndrome)

The worst thing you can do when teaching children with Autism is to do *nothing*.

— Temple Grandin, Ph.D.,
Autism Activist

Mom, I'm normal—everyone else is not.

— William H., Age 9 (Asperger's Syndrome)

I am different, not less.
— Temple Grandin, Ph.D., Autism Activist

I keep waiting on the world to catch up with my son's brain!
— Mother of a child with Autism

*Happiness is not a destination,
it's a part of the journey.*

Happiness...Smiles...Funny Conversations with Kids...

Did you know that it only takes 17 facial muscles to smile as opposed to a frown, which takes 43 facial muscles? Did you know that smiling is scientifically shown to slightly brighten your mood? So, maybe one day when you're feeling down, just smile and know everything is going to be all right.

— Taylor L., Age 12

Mom: Garrett, what are you doing in the pantry?

Garrett: Having an orange slice.

Mom: How many have you had today?

Garrett: One.

Mom: Am I supposed to believe that?

Garrett: Well, I had a lot of them, but I ate them one at a time.

— Garrett M., Age 9

Gabe: Mom, what is this? (Pointing at his plate)

Mom: Mango.

Gabe: Oooh, Italian!

— Gabe L., Age 9

Mom: Carter, you are driving me bananas...seriously.

Carter: Well, Mom, that's okay because I seriously LOVE bananas.

— Carter F., Age 7

Happiness makes me feel like
I am on a giant waterslide!
— Summer S., Age 11

If you are sad, think of manatees,
and your frown will turn around.
— Jordan W., Age 8

Smiling at someone can make their day a whole lot better.

— Jori C., Age 17

Laughing and smiling is one of the
best medicines for any situation.

— Zarea F., Age 16

Mom: Sam, what are you doing in the pantry? You're supposed to be in the shower.

Sam: Getting a granola bar. It's okay, it's small, so it only takes me a few bites because I have a big mouth.

— Sam L., Age 9

A warm smile is the universal language of kindness.
— William Arthur Ward

Mom, I love you with everything in my whole heart and even when you're being mean I am going to tell you that I love you even more, because that is nice.

— Clara F., Age 8

Laughter makes me happy, so
it should make you happy, too.

— Shayla S., Age 11

Have a good mood attitude!

— Damon S., Age 11

Mom after explaining "stranger danger" to her young son:

Mom: Now, Garrett, what do you say when a stranger offers you candy?

Garrett: Please?

— Garrett M., Age 5

Sam: Why are Looney Tunes ™ your favorite, Mom?

Mom: Because it's entertaining, and I loved watching it when I was your age.

Sam: Did they have TV when you were a kid?

— Sam L., Age 9

Smile. Ponder. Change. Live. Laugh. Love.

Trina Dawkins Patterson has a genuine desire to encourage, educate, and empower others, especially youth. She believes a kinder, more compassionate world begins with children. For this reason, she created *Great Inspirations by a Few Great Kids*, a collection of inspirational quotes, poems and short stories written by youth; as well as, *A Tale of Two Cookies*, which is the first in a series of 3 character development books that can be used as teaching tools in the classroom and the home.

Trina is a native of Flint, Michigan. She is the owner of The Cookie Movement, LLC and travels around the United States delivering keynote presentations and facilitating empowerment workshops for women and youth. Mrs. Patterson holds her B.S. in Psychology and M.S. in Administration from Central Michigan University. She received her Montessori Teaching Certification from Midwest Montessori Teacher Training Center. Trina currently lives in Minnesota with her husband and two sons.

You may contact the author at www.thecookiemovement.com or trina@thecookiemovement.com.

Made in the USA
San Bernardino, CA
10 November 2013